W9-BYY-088

Wasps

by Helen Frost

paper wasp

Consulting Editor: Gail Saunders-Smith, Ph.D.

Consultant: Gary A. Dunn, Director of Education,
Young Entomologists' Society

Pebble Books

an imprint of Capstone Press
Mankato, Minnesota

Pebble Books are published by Capstone Press
151 Good Counsel Drive, P.O. Box 669, Mankato, Minnesota 56002
http://www.capstone-press.com

1 2 3 4 5 6 06 05 04 03 02 01

Library of Congress Cataloging-in-Publication Data
Frost, Helen, 1949–
    Wasps/by Helen Frost.
    p. cm.—(Insects)
    Includes bibliographical references (p. 23) and index.
    ISBN 0-7368-0855-8
    1. Wasps—Juvenile literature. [1. Wasps.] I. Title. II. Insects (Mankato, Minn.)
QL565.2 .F76 2001
595.79'8—dc21   00-009675

Summary: Simple text and photographs describe the physical characteristics and
habits of wasps.

Note to Parents and Teachers

The Insects series supports national science standards on units
on the diversity and unity of life. The series shows that animals
have features that help them live in different environments. This
book describes wasps and illustrates their parts and habits. The
photographs support early readers in understanding the text. The
repetition of words and phrases helps early readers learn new
words. This book also introduces early readers to subject-specific
vocabulary words, which are defined in the Words to Know section.
Early readers may need assistance to read some words and to use
the Table of Contents, Words to Know, Read More, Internet Sites,
and Index/Word List sections of the book.

Table of Contents

4

Wasps are flying insects.
They have four thin wings.

a parasitic wasp

waist

Wasps have
a narrow waist.

velvet ant wasp

stinger

Female wasps have
a stinger.

a common wasp

eyes

Wasps have two large eyes made of many lenses.

yellowjacket wasp

jaws

Wasps have strong jaws.

thread-waisted wasp

13

Some wasps live alone.

potter wasp

16

Some wasps live in groups.

yellowjacket wasps

Some wasps build
paper nests.

bald-faced hornet nest

20

Some female wasps lay eggs. Wasp nests have one cell for each egg.

paper wasp and nest

Words to Know

cell—a small space; cells in wasp nests have six sides.

eye—a body part used for seeing; wasps have large eyes made of many small lenses.

female—an animal that can give birth to young animals or lay eggs; female wasps are either queens or workers; most female wasps are workers; queen wasps lay eggs.

nest—a place built to lay eggs and bring up young; queen wasps start building a nest; worker wasps make the nest bigger and stronger; as many as 5,000 wasps live in some wasp nests.

stinger—a sharp, pointed part of an insect that can be used to sting predators; only female wasps have stingers.

Read More

Cutts, David. *I Can Read about Bees and Wasps.* Mahwah, N.J.: Troll, 1998.

Green, Jen. *Wasps.* Nature's Children. Danbury, Conn.: Grolier Educational, 1999.

Scarborough, Kate. *Hornets' Nest.* Watch It Grow. Alexandria, Va.: Time-Life Books, 1997.

Wilsdon, Christina. *National Audobon Society First Field Guide: Insects.* New York: Scholastic, 1998.

Internet Sites

Hymenopera: Vespidae
http://www.ifas.ufl.edu/~eny3005/lab1/Hymenoptera/Vespid.htm

Social Wasps
http://www.ent.iastate.edu/ipm/iiin/bsocialw.html

Wasps
http://www.EnchantedLearning.com/subjects/insects/wasp/Wasp.shtml

Index/Word List

Word Count: 59
Early-Intervention Level: 7

Editorial Credits
Mari C. Schuh, editor; Timothy Halldin, cover designer; Kia Bielke, production designer; Kimberly Danger, photo researcher

Photo Credits
Allen Blake Sheldon, 18
Bill Beatty, 4
Bill Johnson, 1
David Liebman, 6, 8
Michael Redmer/Colephoto, 14
Robert & Linda Mitchell, 20
Visuals Unlimited/R. Calentine, cover; Bill Beatty, 10, 12; Bruce S. Cushing, 16

24

11/02